Answers Explained

Arriving at the Answers to the COMPASS Math Placement Test Sample Questions

COMPASS Answers Explained

CONTENTS

Introduction

"I don't know how to work this problem. Let me see the answers. Oh, I see, the answer is D. Well, that clears everything up."

Does it really?

This document is intended to help you prepare for the COMPASS math placement test; it explains how to arrive at the answers to questions in *COMPASS/ESL Sample Test Questions -- a Guide for Students and Parents -- Mathematics.* This booklet covers both mathematics question booklets: *Numerical Skills/Pre-Algebra, Algebra* (http://www.act.org/compass/sample/pdf/numerical.pdf) and *College Algebra, Geometry, Trigonometry* (http://www.act.org/compass/sample/pdf/geometry.pdf).

Students starting college are often blindsided by placement tests they must pass to be admitted to the math or English courses they want to take. In math, many are placed in developmental courses, which are pretty much a repetition of the algebra that they thought they had gotten overwith in high school. At worst, students may find themselves sitting through a year of non-credit math courses before they can get started on what they came to college for.

Some students really need to take developmental courses. But not everyone. In my private tutoring practice I've seen students fail the placement test, get tutoring, retake the test and pass, and then go on to get As and Bs in higher math courses. Their preparation for the test saved them money and time and left them prepared for higher math courses.

A couple of notes about using this book:

Try to work the problems yourself first, before you look at answers or explanations. That way, the explanations will make more sense to you – if you still need them.

For your reference, statements that generalize beyond the problem being addressed are written in italics.

Do you see errors in this document? Do you want to share your thoughts? I welcome your feedback. Do you live in the Northern Virginia area and are you interested in getting tutoring or joining a group to prepare for the math placement test? Give me a shout at jill@northernvirginialearning.com.

Try to enjoy your studying. (Working with a friend can help with that.) Good luck on the test.

Jill

Numerical Skills/Pre-Algebra

1. $54 - 6 \div 2 + 6$

    The answer is E, 57.

    If you got 30, probably
    you just went left to
    right:

    $54 - 6 \div 2 + 6$

    $48 \div 2 + 6$ **Don't do it this way!**

    $24 + 6$

    30

    But the order-of-operations rules say you
    do multiplication and division **before**
    addition and subtraction.

    There's one division in these
    operations: $6/2$. You can write in

7

parentheses to remind yourself to do that one first. So it's

$54 - (6 \div 2) + 6.$

Then go left to right and it's

$54 - (6 \div 2) + 6 = 54 - 3 + 6 = 51 + 6 = 57.$

These are the rules for the order of operations:

First, do the operations that are within grouping symbols. So, for example,
$6 - (2 + 3) = 6 - 5 = 1.$

Note: A fraction bar is a grouping symbol. So in, for example, $\dfrac{3 \times 2}{5 \times 4}$, the numerator $3 \times 2 = 6$ and the denominator $5 \times 4 = 20$ are calculated separately before the fraction division is carried out.

Call this step "P," for "parentheses."

Next, carry out any exponentiation. Call this step "E."

Next come multiplication and division. The two have equal status, so go from left to right. Call this step "MD."

Finally come addition and subtraction, which have equal status, so go from left to right. Call this step "AS."

If you put the letters together, you can form a mnemonic: PEMDAS.

2. You are asked to find the difference between 24 and -8.

   To subtract a negative number from a positive number, make the negative number positive and then add the numbers.

   $24 - (-8) = 24 + 8 = 32$

   If you have trouble remembering the rules for addition and subtraction involving negative numbers, think of a number line.

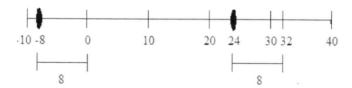

   The space between -8 and 24 represents the difference between the two numbers. That space is equal to the distance from -8 to 0 plus the difference from 0 to 24, or 8 + 24, or 32.

3. You're asked to find the denominator of the fraction that results from

$\left(\dfrac{3}{4} - \dfrac{2}{3}\right) + \left(\dfrac{1}{2} + \dfrac{1}{3}\right)$. To find it, you pretty

much have to carry out the operations. *To add or subtract fractions, convert the fractions so that they have a common denominator and then add the numerators.*

First carry out the operations within parentheses. The first step to finding $\dfrac{3}{4} - \dfrac{2}{3}$ is to find a common denominator for the two fractions. The smallest number that is divisible by both 4 and 3 is 12, so that's the common denominator. Convert the fractions to a common denominator by multiplying by 1 in the form of 3 divided by itself or 4 divided by itself:

$\dfrac{3}{4} \times \dfrac{3}{3} = \dfrac{9}{12}; \dfrac{2}{3} \times \dfrac{4}{4} = \dfrac{8}{12}$. So

$\dfrac{3}{4} - \dfrac{2}{3} = \dfrac{9}{12} - \dfrac{8}{12} = \dfrac{1}{12}$. This fraction cannot be reduced.

Same sort of thing with the second parentheses. The least common denominator is 6.

$\dfrac{1}{2} + \dfrac{1}{3} = \dfrac{1}{2} \times \dfrac{3}{3} + \dfrac{1}{3} \times \dfrac{2}{2} = \dfrac{3}{6} + \dfrac{2}{6} = \dfrac{5}{6}$.

Now you've got to add two fractions with denominators of 12 and 6. The least common denominator for the two is 12, and the operation becomes $\dfrac{1}{12} + \dfrac{5}{6} \times \dfrac{2}{2} = \dfrac{1}{12} + \dfrac{10}{12} = \dfrac{11}{12}$. This fraction is irreducible, and the answer is 12.

Alternatively, you could start by removing all the parentheses and look for one common denominator for all four fractions. You should get the same answer and it comes out to about the same amount of work either way.

4.   First do what's in the parentheses; then do the addition and subtraction.

The second set of parentheses: *To multiply fractions, multiply numerator by numerator and denominator by denominator:*
$\dfrac{4}{5} \times \dfrac{5}{6} = \dfrac{20}{30} = \dfrac{2}{3}$.

The first set of parentheses: *To divide fractions, you multiply the first fraction by the reciprocal of the second.* So $\dfrac{2}{3} \div \dfrac{3}{4}$ becomes $\dfrac{2}{3} \times \dfrac{4}{3}$ and that is equal to $\dfrac{8}{9}$.

Now you just have to pick up the pieces:
You've got $\frac{1}{2} + \frac{8}{9} - \frac{2}{3}$. You need a common denominator:

$$\frac{1}{2} + \frac{8}{9} - \frac{2}{3} = \frac{1}{2} \times \frac{9}{9} + \frac{8}{9} \times \frac{2}{2} - \frac{2}{3} \times \frac{6}{6} = \frac{9}{18} + \frac{16}{18} - \frac{12}{18}$$

Adding the numerators gives $\frac{13}{18}$.

5. Any confusion you feel upon reading this question may come as a result of seeing two of the measurements in fractions and one in a decimal. You need to choose one way. Which one is better? You're asked for the answer as a decimal; you can see that by a glance at the answers. So convert those fractions into decimals and see what you get.

$\frac{3}{4} = .75$ (Think of money. Three quarters are worth seventy-five cents.) So

$7\frac{3}{4} = 7.75$

$\frac{1}{2} = .5$, so $6\frac{1}{2} = 6.5$

Now you just need to add 7.75 + 17.85 + 6.5. *To add decimal numbers, line up the decimal points and add corresponding decimal values, carrying as appropriate:*

7.75

17.85

6.50

_____

That adds up to 32.1.

6.   It's a word problem and your first job is
      to get your arms around it. You are asked
      for the difference in cost **per person**
      between two deals. The first deal is clear:
      $18.50 per person. The cost per person of
      the second deal is what you have to
      figure out. Five people are getting tickets
      for $80.00. That's $80/5 = $16 per ticket.
      Now you just need to find the difference
      between the two: $18.50 - $16.00 = $2.50.

      Each person would save $2.50.

      It would have been easy to answer
      mistakenly with the **total** amount saved
      by the group. *It's a good idea to reread word
      problems just before you fill in the answer, to
      make sure you're answering the right
      question.*

7. You're asked to add two numbers and express the result in scientific notation.

   First, add the numbers: 20,000 + 3,400,000 = 3,420,000.

   Now, express the result in scientific notation: Move the decimal point so that there is just one nonzero digit to its left. Then remove any zeros at the end.

   Moving the decimal point effectively changes the number's value, dividing or multiplying it by a multiple of 10. You need to undo that. What am I talking about? In 3,420,000, move the decimal point to one place to the right of the first digit and remove zeros at the end: 3.42. In doing this, you have divided 3,420,000 by 1,000,000. You need to undo that by multiplying by 1,000,000, which is 10^6. So you get 3.42×10^6.

8. "$4 < \sqrt{x} < 9$" is a compound inequality. It's really two inequalities expressed in one statement. As long as all the expressions involved are positive, as they are here, you can square everything and the statement is still true. In other words, for positive values, if $a < b < c$, then $a^2 < b^2 < c^2$. (This may not work if some

14

values involved are negative.) For the example given, that means $16 < x < 81$. And that's the answer.

9. Solve for x by isolating x. Multiply both sides of the equation by 8 to get $x = \dfrac{8 \times 9}{6} => x = \dfrac{72}{6}$. Simplifying $\dfrac{72}{6}$ gives $x = 12$.

10. The cost of a bag of apples will be in proportion to the cost of one apple and to the number of apples in the bag. So the cost of a bag of x apples – b – is kx, where $k,$ a name for the cost of one apple, is a constant. So $kx = b$. You can solve for k by dividing both sides by x; $k = b/x$.

The cost of a bag of y apples – call it c – is ky, where k is the same number as for the bag of x apples. But you can't give the answer in terms of k (that is, with a k in it), because, well, k is just something I made up. Instead you can substitute for k terms that you were given; $k = \dfrac{b}{x}; c = ky = \dfrac{by}{x}$. And that's the answer.

11. Twelve students are 25% (or one-fourth) of the class. So the full class membership is $4 \times 12 = 48$.

COMPASS Answers Explained

Another way to look at it: These twelve are 25% of the class, so $12 = .25n$, where n is the number of students in the class. Divide both sides by .25 and you get

$12 = .25n$

$$\frac{12}{.25} = n$$

$n = 48$

12. These kids take a lot of math!

The students who took fewer than six math courses are the whole graduating class minus the 75% who took at least eight math courses, minus the 60% of the remaining students who took six or seven math courses.

Let's look at "60% of the remaining students." "The remaining students," the students that remain after you subtract the initial 75%, are 25%. Sixty percent of those are $.60 \times .25 = .15$, or 15% of the whole graduating class. That means 15% of the graduating class took six or seven math courses.

The total number of students who took at least six math courses is the sum of those who took at least eight (75%) and those who took six or seven (15%). That's 90%.

Those who took fewer than six courses are the rest: 100% - 90% = 10%.

It's 10%.

13. Well, how did Adam get that wrong average in the first place? The average test score would be the sum of all test scores divided by the number of tests. You don't know the sum; let's call it s.

Then the wrong average is $\dfrac{s}{6} = 84$.

Solving for s by multiplying both sides by 6 gives $s = 6 \times 84$. (You could multiply it out but it's usually easier to leave the calculations until the end.) The correct average is $\dfrac{s}{7}$. Substituting the value you found for s gives $(6 \times 84)/7$ and that is equal to 12. 12 points off his average just like that.

14. You're asked for a weighted average.

The average for all students would be the sum of all students' scores divided by the number of students. You don't know every student's score, but you do the average scores of two groups of students. Since the average of the juniors' scores, 80, is the sum of the juniors' scores (call it J) divided by the number of juniors, the sum of the juniors' scores is the juniors' average score times the number of juniors: $J = 80 \times 35$. Likewise for the seniors, the sum of their scores, call it S, is $S = 70 \times 15$. The sum of all students' scores is the sum of these — $J + S = (80 \times 35) + (70 \times 15)$ — and the average for all 50 students is the sum of all scores divided by 50: average $=$

$$\frac{(J + S)}{50} = \frac{\left[(80 \times 35) + (70 \times 15)\right]}{50} = 77.$$

Algebra

1. I could just tell you to substitute -3 for x, but then you might wonder why you're bothering to read this. So instead I'll tell you a way that may be easier. If this "easier" way gives you a headache, you can always just substitute.

    Factor the numerator of $\dfrac{x^2 - 1}{x + 1}$ and you get $\dfrac{(x + 1)(x - 1)}{x + 1}$. $x + 1$ shows up in both

18

the numerator and the denominator, so you can cancel it out. (Caution: This does not work for values of x that make the denominator 0. But we will not be messing with $x = 1$, the only value of x that has that problem.) Then you're left with $x - 1$ as the value of the expression. If $x = -3$, then $x - 1 = -4$, and that's the answer.

2. You need to find *THR*. You're given a formula for *THR* that includes the terms *RHR* and *MHR*. Then you're given *RHR* -- 54 beats per minute -- but not *MHR*. Instead, you're told that *MHR* equals 220 minus age. You can put all that together into:

$$THR = RHR + .65\big[(220 - age) - RHR\big]$$

Age is 43 and *RHR* is 54. So
$$THR = 54 + .65\big[(220 - 43) - 54\big]$$
$$THR = 54 + .65(123)$$

THR is about 134.

3. Take it in steps.
    Subtract *a* from 220: $220 - a$.
    Take 75% of that value: $.75 \times (220 - a)$.

That's the answer.

4. *Distance* = *time* X *rate*. Break it into pieces. The time, 8 hours, at the first speed, multiplied by the first speed, x, plus the time at the other speed, 7 hours, multiplied by the other speed, 325 mph, equals the entire time, 15 hours, times the average speed, 350 mph. In equation form that's $8x + 7 \times 325 = 15 \times 350$.

5. You have to subtract $-6a - 3b$ from $3a + 4b$. The tricky part is subtracting the negative. But you know the rules: *To subtract a negative, change the subtraction to addition and the negative to a positive.* So $3a + 4b - (-6a - 3b)$ is equal to $3a + 4b + (6a + 3b) = 9a + 7b$.

6. You can add only like terms. Like terms are terms that contain the same variables, to the same powers. The only like terms in the expressions you are given are $2a^2b^2$ and a^2b^2: Both contain the variables a and b, each to the second power. $2a^2b^2 + a^2b^2 = 3a^2b^2$ and the other two terms do not change, so the final answer is $3a^2b + -ab^2 + 3a^2b^2$.

7. You have to factor $x^2 - x - 20$ into two binomials, something of the form $(x + m)(x + n)$, where m and n are numbers you have to find.

What do you know about m and n? Multiply $(x + m)(x + n)$ and you get $x^2 + (m + n)x + mn$. So in our example, $m + n$ is equal to the multiplier of x, -1; and mn is equal to the constant term, -20. You need to find factors of -20 that add up to -1. The negative product, -20, tells you that one factor is positive and one is negative. The negative sum, -1, tells you that the negative number is greater in magnitude than the positive one. Play around with some factors of -20 and you'll find that the only pair that works is -5 and 4. So the factors of $x^2 - x - 20$ are $(x - 5)$ and $(x + 4)$. Look for one of those factors in the answer list: $x - 5$. Multiply back to check.

8. Nother factoring problem. See #7. If, again, you call the binomials $x + m$ and $x + n$, and multiply them to get $x^2 + (m + n)x + mn$, then this time $m + n = -5$ and $mn = -6$. Again, as in #7, the negative product ($mn = -6$) tells you that m and n are opposite in sign and the negative sum ($m + n = -5$) tells you the negative number is greater in magnitude than the positive one. The only integer factors of -6 that add up to -5 are -6 and 1, so the factors are $x - 6$ and $x + 1$.

9. $2(x-5)=-11$; divide both sides by 2 to
    get $x-5=\dfrac{-11}{2}$; add 5 to both sides to get
    $x=5-\dfrac{11}{2}$; use a common denominator (2)
    to get $x=5-\dfrac{11}{2}=\dfrac{10}{2}-\dfrac{11}{2}$; subtract the
    fractions to get $x=-\dfrac{1}{2}$.

10. To start, simplify by multiplying by 10,
    the common denominator. Then all the
    fractions will go away.

$$\frac{4}{5}+\frac{-3}{10}=x+1\frac{1}{2}$$
$$\frac{4}{5}\times10+\frac{-3}{10}\times10=10x+\frac{3}{2}\times10$$
$$\frac{40}{5}+\frac{-30}{10}=x+15$$

Now simplify:

$8-3=10x+15$.

Now it doesn't look so bad. Gather like
terms and solve for x.

$$5 = 10x + 15$$
$$-10 = 10x$$
$$x = -1$$

11. You have to simplify the fraction $\dfrac{16r^3tz^5}{-4rt^3z^2}$.

Cancel constants. 16 in the numerator cancels with -4 in the denominator, yielding -4 in the numerator. You'll get $\dfrac{-4r^3tz^5}{rt^3z^2}$.

How does r^3 in the numerator relate to r in the denominator? Consider:

$r^3 = r \times r \times r$. So $\dfrac{r^3}{r} = \dfrac{r \times r \times r}{r}$, or r^2. In fact, *any variable* n *to a power* a, *divided by* n *to a power* b, *is equal to* n *to the power of* a-b *as long as* n *is not equal to 0.* $\dfrac{n^a}{n^b} = n^{a-b}$ So for the z term, $\dfrac{z^5}{z^2} = z^{5-2} = z^3$.

But what about the t term? $\dfrac{t^1}{t^3} = t^{1-3} = t^{-2}$. A negative exponent. Can that be?

Yes and no. *A negative exponent is valid, but it has no place in a simplified expression.* Answers are usually expected to be given in simplified form. That's why none of the answers listed contains a negative exponent.

But you've got one. What to do? Remember that *a change in an exponent's sign is equivalent to a flip over the fraction bar* -- and a change in the exponent's sign **coupled with** a flip over the fraction bar amounts to no change at all, just as multiplying twice by -1 amounts to no change at all. So $t^{-2} = \dfrac{1}{t^2}$.

Put it all together and you have $\dfrac{-4r^2z^3}{t^2}$

12. This is another problem in simplifying radicals. Note that none of the answer choices has a radical in its denominator. That's because *simplified fractions don't have radicals in their denominators*.

The original denominator contains radicals. How do you get rid of them?

You multiply by the conjugate. What's that? For an expression $a + \sqrt{b}$, the conjugate is $a - \sqrt{b}$. Why multiply by the conjugate? Watch what happens:

$$\left(a + \sqrt{b}\right)\left(a - \sqrt{b}\right) = a^2 - a\sqrt{b} + a\sqrt{b} - \left(\sqrt{b}\right)^2 - a^2b$$

24

The radicals are gone.

Apply this method to the problem. You need to clear the denominator of radicals, so find the denominator's conjugate: $3\sqrt{x} + \sqrt{y}$. Then multiply the expression by 1 in the form of the conjugate divided by itself:

$$\frac{\left(\sqrt{x}\right)}{\left(3\sqrt{x} - \sqrt{y}\right)} \cdot \frac{\left(3\sqrt{x} + \sqrt{y}\right)}{\left(3\sqrt{x} + \sqrt{y}\right)}$$

$$= \frac{\left(3\left(\sqrt{x}\right)^2 + \sqrt{x}\sqrt{y}\right)}{\left(9\left(\sqrt{x}\right)^2 + 3\sqrt{x}\sqrt{y} - 3\sqrt{x}\sqrt{y} - \left(\sqrt{y}\right)^2\right)}$$

$$= \frac{\left(3x + \sqrt{xy}\right)}{\left(9x - y\right)}$$

13. Factor the numerator. Then maybe something will cancel and you can get a simpler expression.

   How do you factor the numerator? See #7. Set the expression equal to $(x + m)(x + n)$, which equals $x^2 + (m + n)x + mn$. $m + n$, the multiplier of x, is equal to 12; mn, the constant term, is equal to 32. The integers m and n have both a positive product and a positive sum, so they must both be positive. Try some combinations of factors of 32 – there are only so many: 1 and 32; 2

and 16; 4 and 8. That's it: $4 \times 8 = 32$; $4 + 8 = 12$. So m and n are 4 and 8; $x + m = x + 4$; $x + n = x + 8$; and $x^2 + 12x + 32 = (x+4)(x+8)$.

Put that back into the rational expression:
$$\frac{x^2 + 12x + 32}{x + 4} = \frac{(x+4)(x+8)}{x+4} = x + 8.$$

Why does it matter that x not equal -4? If x = -4, then the denominator equals 0, and the expression is undefined.

14.   We're still factoring.

How can you factor $9 - x^2$?

For any difference of two squares, $a^2 - b^2$, the factored form is $(a+b)(a-b)$. $9 - x^2$ is a difference of two squares; its factors are $3 + x$ and $3 - x$. So $\dfrac{9 - x^2}{x - 3}$ becomes $\dfrac{(3+x)(3-x)}{x-3}$. Are there any common factors between the numerator and the denominator? No? Are you sure? Try this: Multiply the numerator twice by -1. That won't change the expression's value, right? Here's how to do it: Multiply both the entire expression, and the term $3 - x$, by -1. That gives $-(3+x)(-3+x)$ for the numerator. Now, using the commutative property of addition, rewrite $-3+x$ as $x-3$. Then the numerator is $-(3+x)(x-3)$ and the expression is $\dfrac{-(3+x)(3-x)}{x-3}$.

The term $x-3$ appears in both the numerator and the denominator. Can you cancel it? You can, as long as $x-3$ is not equal to 0. And you know it's not, because you are told that $x < -3$.

So the simplified expression is $-(3+x)$, which is equal to $-x-3$.

15. *When a line's equation is in slope-intercept form – $y = mx + b$ – you can read the slope right off the equation. It's m.* So put this line into slope-intercept form. That is, solve for y: $2x + 3y + 6 = 0$; therefore, $3y = -2x - 6$; therefore, $y = -\dfrac{2}{3}x - 2$. The slope is -2/3.

16. The line you're looking for is perpendicular to the line $x = 2$. The line $x = 2$ is vertical. So the line you're looking for is horizontal. That means the y value of all points on the line will be the same as the y value of the given point: 1.

Now you just need to find the *x* value. The perpendicular bisector will cut line segment *AB* into two pieces of equal length, so it will be halfway in-between. The point (2, 1) is halfway between the given point, (-4, 1), and another point the same distance to the right of (2, 1) as (-4, 1) is to the left of (2, 1). That would be 6 (that is, 2– (-4)) units to the right of (2, 1). That's the point you need: (8, 1).

College Algebra

1. *In a geometric sequence, each term is equal to the term before it multiplied by a constant.* In this case, as you can see, each term is equal to the term before it multiplied by - 1/4. So the next term is equal to the last term given –

   $-\dfrac{1}{4}$ – multiplied by $-\dfrac{1}{4}$. That is,

   $$-\dfrac{1}{4} \cdot -\dfrac{1}{4} = \dfrac{1}{16}.$$

2. The maximum output is either the amount that Process A can produce, or the amount that Process B can produce, in 7 days. Until

you do the calculations, you don't know which will produce more – so you have to calculate the outputs of both processes.

To find the output at 7 days, set t equal to 7.

For Process A, $A(t) = t^2 + 2t$

$A(7) = 7^2 + 2 \times 7 = 49 + 14 = 63$

For Process A, 63 tons can be produced.

For Process B, $B(t) = 10t$

$B(7) = 10 \times 7 = 70$

For Process B, 70 tons can be produced. That's more than the 63 tons from Process A, so it is the maximum. It is the answer.

3. This question is about composite functions. Usually we talk about functions of x; *a composite function is a function of a function.*

f is a function of x, and g is a function of f.

From the first table, you can see that $f(3)$ is 2. (That is, when $x = 3$, $f = 2$.) In the next part, $f(3)$, which is 2, becomes x. $g(2) = -3$, and that is the final answer.

4. *A fractional exponent is a root. For example,*

$4^{\frac{1}{2}} = \sqrt{4}$. *So* $x^{\frac{1}{2}} y^{\frac{2}{3}} z^{\frac{5}{6}} = \left(\sqrt{x}\right)\left(\sqrt[3]{y^2}\right)\left(\sqrt[6]{z^5}\right)$. *But that doesn't look like any of the expressions on the list – each of them has only one radical sign, with all the variables underneath it.*

You can iron it out by giving the exponents a common denominator:

$$x^{\frac{1}{2}} y^{\frac{2}{3}} z^{\frac{5}{6}} = x^{\frac{3}{6}} y^{\frac{4}{6}} z^{\frac{5}{6}} = \sqrt[6]{x^3}\sqrt[6]{y^4}\sqrt[6]{z^5} = \sqrt[6]{x^3 y^4 z^5}.$$

5. To add matrices, add each of the elements of one matrix to the corresponding element of the other. To subtract matrices, subtract each element of the second matrix from the corresponding element of the first.

$$A - B = \begin{bmatrix} 2 & -4 \\ 6 & 0 \end{bmatrix} - \begin{bmatrix} -2 & 4 \\ -6 & 0 \end{bmatrix} = \begin{bmatrix} 4 & -8 \\ 12 & 0 \end{bmatrix}$$

For example, the term in the upper left-hand corner of the difference matrix (the result) is equal to the difference of the terms in the upper left-hand corners of the two matrices given: $2 - (-2) = 4$.

6. The original function is $f(x) = 2^x$; with $f(g(x))$ you are looking for $2^{(g(x))}$ for various functions g.

For positive values of x, the exponential function, of which 2^x is an example, is an always-increasing function. That is, a higher value of x means a higher value of $f(x)$: If $a > b$ then $2^a > 2^b$.

You know also that $c > 1$ and that $x > 1$.

Let's look at the answer choices and compare them.

A. $g(x) = cx$. Then $f(g(x)) = 2^{cx}$. As x increases, cx increases and 2^{cx} also increases.

B. $g(x) = \dfrac{c}{x}$ Then $f(g(x)) = 2^{\frac{c}{x}}$. As x increases, c/x decreases and $2^{\frac{c}{x}}$ decreases. When $x=1$, $\dfrac{c}{x} = cx$, so when $x > 1$, the case we are considering, $\dfrac{c}{x} < c$ and $2^{\frac{c}{x}} < 2^{cx}$. The result for answer A is greater than the result for answer B, and answer B is out.

C. Since $c > 1$, $\dfrac{x}{c} < cx$, so $2^{\frac{x}{c}} < 2^{cx}$ and of the functions you've looked at, A is still the greatest.

D. Since $c > 1$, $x - c < cx$, and $2^{x-c} < 2^{cx}$. This choice is out and A is still in the lead.

31

E. Now it's down to A v. E. What's greater for all $x > 1$, 2^{cx} or $2^{\log_c x}$?

Consider one value of x. For what value of x do you know $\log_c x$? If $x = c$, then $\log_c x = \log_c c = 1$. (Remember: $\log_a a = 1$ for all $a > 0$ and $a \neq 1$.) Compare this with cx: For $x = c$, $cx = x^2$. Since $x > 1$, $cx = x^2 > 1$, so $cx > \log_c x$ and $2^{cx} > 2^{\log_c x}$, at least for $x = c$.

But you're asked to make a statement for all $x > 1$. Can you compare 2^{cx} with $2^{\log_c x}$ for values of x other than c? Then again, do you have to do that? If $2^{cx} > 2^{\log_c x}$ for one value of x, as we have found, then it can't be true that $2^{\log_c x} > 2^{cx}$ for all values of x. So answer E is out and answer A must be correct.

7. Let's say $x = 0$. Then
$f(x + y) = f(x) + f(y)$ (from the problem statement); $f(x + y) = f(0) + f(y)$ and $x + y = y$ (because $x = 0$), so
$f(x + y) = f(y) = f(0) + f(y)$. So $f(0)$ must equal 0.

8.   This one is not as bad as it looks.

When you come to a problem that looks like it will involve a lot of calculation, look for a pattern that will save steps. Often you can find one by playing with the information you've got, or just by starting to do the detail work.

If $i = \sqrt{-1}$, then $i^2 = -1$, $i^3 = -\sqrt{-1} = -i$, $i^4 = i^2 \times i^2 = -1 \times -1 = 1$, and $i^5 = \sqrt{-1} \times 1$. That last one, i^5, is just the same as i – so i^6 is the same as i^2, and there is a pattern: Every fourth power, the series will repeat.

You're asked to add. OK, let's start adding and see what happens. i, i^2, i^3, and i^4 are equal, respectively, to $\sqrt{-1}$, -1, $-\sqrt{-1}$, and 1. Rearranging, you get $\sqrt{-1} + \left(-\sqrt{-1}\right) + 1 - 1$. So the first four terms cancel each other out. And the series repeats – for example, $i^5 + i^6 + i^7 + i^8 = i + i^2 + i^3 + i^4$. Every following group of four will do the same thing. For example, $i^5 + i^6 + i^7 + i^8$. Etc. That will continue until you get to an incomplete group, a group missing one or two or three elements.

Notice that each group of four ends with a power that is divisible by 4. The series you're asked to look at ends with a 23rd power – a power that is one less than a number that is divisible by 4. The last number in the group of 4, i^4, is equal to 1. So the sum of the last three terms in the series is equal to the sum of all four terms – 0 – minus 1, for the last term; the sum is -1. Because the rest of the series is complete groups that cancel each other out, the sum of incomplete groups is the sum of the whole series.

The answer is -1.

9. This is a tough problem. And when the going gets tough, the tough mathematician gets naming things.

There are two things you need to know: the difference between each term and the next (4 in the example) and the number of terms. Let's call the first d and the second n. If you knew either of these, you could find the other one pretty easily. For example, if you knew how many terms there are, you could figure that the difference between terms is the length of the series (136-3=133) divided by the number of gaps between terms, that is, the number of terms minus one. But you don't know how many terms there are.

What do you know about d and n? You know that $3 + (n-1) \times d = 136$ – that is, the first term, plus the number of gaps times the size of the gaps – is equal to the last term. And you know that

$$3 + (3 + d) + (3 + d + d) + \ldots + (3 + (n - 1) \times d) = 1,39($$

That's the sum. Pretty clunky expression. Can you say something more manageable? The sum is the **average** value in the series times the **number** of values in the series. And you can easily find the average value: It's the sum of the lowest and highest numbers, all divided by 2. (The average can be found this way because the numbers are spaced evenly.)

Let's put that together:

Average value in the series: $\dfrac{136 + 3}{2} = \dfrac{139}{2}$

Sum of terms in the series: average times number of terms $= \dfrac{139}{2} \times n$

Sum of terms in the series: 1,390 (from problem statement)

Set the two values for average equal to each other and solve for n:

$$\frac{139}{2} n = 1,390$$

$$n = \frac{(1,390)(2)}{139}$$

So there are 20 terms in the series.

You still need to find d, the difference between terms. The number of spaces between terms is equal to the number of terms, n, minus one. The range of the series – the highest number minus the lowest – divided by the number of spaces is equal to the distance between terms. That is, $d = \dfrac{(136 - 3)}{19} = 7$. So the distance between terms is 7. Since it was given that the first term was 3, the next two terms are 10 and 17. That's answer A.

In case that's not to your liking, here's an alternate method: Inspect the answers and rule out whatever you can.

Answers A, B, and D meet the requirements: their terms are, as the question states, "equally spread out." C and E are not, so they're out.

Start with answer B, the middle one of the ones remaining, and list the elements: 3, 23, 43. The difference between consecutive terms is 20; keep going: 63, 83 . . .. All the terms end in 3, so the last term can't be 136. So B is out.

Now try answer choice D. The last term shown, 136, is the required last term in the series. Does it work? The sum of all the terms in the series is supposed to be 1,390. Add together the terms in answer D and you get just 208 1/2. So that can't be right.

That leaves A. You are given 3, 10, and 17. The difference between terms is 7. Keep on adding 7s until you get to 136: 3, 10, 17, 24, 31, 38, 45, 52, 59, 66, 73, 80, 87, 94, 101, 108, 115, 122, 129, and 136. Bingo. Add 'em up, or, as in the first method for this problem, multiply the average by the number of terms. There are 20 terms. Because the terms are evenly spaced, the average of the series is the average of the first and last terms: $\frac{3+136}{2} = \frac{139}{2}$. And $\left(\frac{139}{2}\right)(20) = 1,390$. Check. Answer A is correct.

Geometry

1. When two parallel lines are cut by a transversal, angles of two different sizes are formed (unless the transversal is perpendicular to the parallel lines, in which case all the angles formed will be the same size). You are asked to find a set of angles that are all the same size.

   Angles *a* and *b* are *vertical* angles. *Vertical angles are equal in measure.*

   Angles *b* and *d* are *alternate interior* angles. *When two parallel lines are cut by a transversal, the alternate interior angles formed are equal in measure.*

   Angles *c* and *e* are *corresponding* angles, meaning *c* bears the same relationship to one line (*m* in this case) as *e* bears to the other (*n*). The same is true for angles *a* and *d*. *When two parallel lines are cut by a transversal, the corresponding angles formed are equal.*

So angle *a* is equal in measure to angle *b*, and angle *b* is equal in measure to angle *d*. The correct answer is angles *a*, *b*, and *d*.

2. This triangle is isosceles – that is, it has two equal sides. *In an isosceles triangle, the angles opposite the equal sides are equal.* So angles *B* and *C* are equal in measure. Then, since the sum of the angle measures in any triangle is 180 degrees, $40 + 2x = 180$ and $x = 70$. So angles *B* and *C* each measure 70. The angle you need is the supplement to angle *ACB* – the angle that together with angle *ACB* adds up to 180. That would be $180 - 70 = 110$.

3. The perimeter is the sum of the lengths of the fence sections. Each section except the diagonal one is 10 feet long. Count the number of sections and multiply by 10. There are twenty 10-foot sections, so the perimeter is 200 feet plus the diagonal. How long is the diagonal? Longer than one of the other sections, shorter than two: somewhere between 10 and 20 feet. So the whole perimeter is between 210 and 220 feet. The only answer choice that works is $P > 210$.

4. *The area of a rectangle is its length times its width.* So the area of this rectangle is 16 times 9, or 144. *The area of a square is the length of a side squared.* So the length of a side of the

COMPASS Answers Explained

square you are looking for is square root of
144. The square root of 144 is 12.

5. *The Pythagorean Theorem says the square of the
length of the hypotenuse of a right triangle is
equal to the sum of the squares of the legs.* If the
hypotenuse is c and the legs are a and b, then
$c^2 = a^2 + b^2$. You are looking for b.

$b^2 = c^2 - a^2$; $b = \sqrt{c^2 - a^2}$. In this case, $c = 6$
and $a = 3$, so
$b = \sqrt{c^2 - a^2} = \sqrt{6^2 - 3^2} = \sqrt{36 - 9} = \sqrt{27}$.

Note that $\sqrt{27}$ is not on the answer list.
That's because, as usual, all the answers on
the list are in simplified form, but $\sqrt{27}$ is
not in simplified form. How do you
simplify it?

$27 = 3 \times 3 \times 3 = 3^2 \times 3$, so
$\sqrt{27} = \sqrt{3^2 \times 3} = \sqrt{3^2} \times \sqrt{3} = 3\sqrt{3}$ – and that's
answer choice B.

6. The 30° angle covers $\dfrac{30}{360} = \dfrac{1}{12}$ of the circle.

So does the arc that it subtends. So 6 is $\dfrac{1}{12}$ of
the circumference, and the entire
circumference is $6 \times 12 = 72$. You need to
find the radius. $C = 2\pi r$ where C is the

40

circumference and r is the radius.

$$r = \frac{C}{2\pi} = \frac{72}{2\pi} = \frac{36}{\pi}.$$

7. The *volume of a rectangular box is equal to its length times its width times its height.* In the case of the first box in this example that's $2 \times 6 \times 10 = 120$ in^3. The area of the new base is $3 \times 5 = 15$ in^2. The height is the volume, 120 in^3, divided by the new base, 15 in^2. That's
120 in^3 / 15 in^2 = 8 in.

8. The area that remains of the large circle is the whole area of the large circle minus the area of the small circle. *The area of a circle is equal to π times the square of its radius.* You can see that the radius of the small circle is 5, but what is the radius of the large circle? Note that the diameter of the small circle is the radius of the large circle, so the radius of the large circle is 10. Then the area of the large circle is $\pi \times 10^2 = 100\pi$ and that of the small circle is $\pi \times 5^2 = 25\pi$, and the difference between them is $100\pi - 25\pi = 75\pi$.

9. *The area of a trapezoid is its height times the average of the bases.* The height of the trapezoid in the problem is 4. Its top base is 10 units long. What is the length of its bottom base?

The length of the bottom base is 10 units plus the extension on the left beyond the top base as well as the extension on the right beyond the top base. Note that this is an isosceles trapezoid: its two sides have the same length. So those extensions to the left and right are equal.

Look at the triangle on the left. It is a right triangle, with a hypotenuse of 5 and one leg of length 4. By the Pythagorean Theorem, the length of the remaining leg is $\sqrt{5^2 - 4^2} = \sqrt{25 - 16} = \sqrt{9} = 3$. So the length of the longer base is 10 units plus two extensions, each of length 3: $10 + 3 + 3 = 16$.

The area, then, is $4 \times \dfrac{10 + 16}{2} = 4 \times \dfrac{26}{2} = 52$.

10. This is an exercise in similar triangles. You know they're similar, because they share one angle (the angle that is 15 feet from the streetlight) and there is another set of angles that have the same measure: The streetlight and the tree both meet the ground at right angles. That's two angles, enough to establish similarity.

In similar triangles, corresponding sides have proportional lengths. The height of the streetlight divided by the height of the tree is equal to the distance from the streetlight's base to the end of the tree's shadow, all divided by the length of the tree's shadow. That is: $\dfrac{18}{6} = \dfrac{15 + x}{x}$, where x is the length you're looking for. Solving for x gives $x = 7.5$.

Note: It may be tempting to say $\dfrac{18}{6} = \dfrac{15}{x}$ and leave x out the numerator. But that would mean substituting just a piece of the base – 15 – where the whole base – 15+x – is called for.

11. *A triangle's area is equal to one-half the product of its base and its height.* But what is the height of triangle *DEG*?

    *A triangle's height is a line segment that runs from one vertex to the opposite side and is perpendicular to the side it intersects. A triangle's height does **not** have to fall within the triangle.* Side *GF* is the height, side *DE* is the base, and the area, *A*, is $A = \dfrac{1}{2} \times 12 \times 10 = 60$.

Trigonometry

1. You are given a right triangle, you are told the length of its hypotenuse and the measure of one angle other than the right angle, you are given trig functions for that angle, and you are asked for the length of one other side.

   Look for a trig function that involves both the side you need to know – that is, side *BC*, the side opposite the given angle – and the hypotenuse. $\sin A = \dfrac{opposite}{hypotenuse}$, so use sine.

   Since $\sin A = \dfrac{opposite}{hypotenuse}$,
   $opposite = \sin A \times hypotenuse$. Substitute the values you are given:
   sin *A* = 0.866 and the length of the hypotenuse is 8, so the length of side *BC* is $0.866 \times 8 = 6.93$.

2. $\sin = \dfrac{opposite}{hypotenuse}$, $\cos A = \dfrac{adjacent}{hypotenuse}$, and
   $\sin A = \dfrac{opposite}{hypotenuse}$, so $\tan = {\sin}/{\cos}$.

And $\tan = \dfrac{opposite}{adjacent} = \dfrac{\dfrac{opposite}{hypotenuse}}{\dfrac{adjacent}{hypotenuse}} = \dfrac{\sin}{\cos}$, so

$\tan = \dfrac{\sin}{\cos}$.

Then $\tan\alpha = \dfrac{\sin\alpha}{\cos\alpha} = \dfrac{\dfrac{12}{13}}{\dfrac{5}{13}} = \dfrac{12}{5}$

3. You are given an angle's sine and asked to find its cosine.

   Consider a right triangle with an angle whose sine is 1/2.

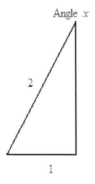

Angle x's sine is equal to the length of the opposite leg divided by the length of the triangle's hypotenuse, so if the length of the opposite leg is 1, then the length of the hypotenuse is 2, for a sine of $1/2$. Angle x's cosine is equal to the length of the other leg divided by the hypotenuse.

What's the length of the other leg? You can use the Pythagorean Theorem to find it. If you call the length of the other leg s, then

$$2^2 = 1^2 + s^2$$
$$s^2 = 4 - 1$$
$$s^2 = 3$$
$$s = \sqrt{3}$$

Then the cosine of x is equal to

$$\frac{s}{hypotenuse} = \frac{\sqrt{3}}{2}.$$

4. Call the unknown length x. You are asked to find the length of one leg; the length of the other is 1.3. So both legs are involved and the hypotenuse is not. The trig function that works with both legs but not the hypotenuse is tangent.

The tangent of 57° is equal to the side opposite the 57° angle divided by the unknown side.

$$\tan 57 = \frac{1.3}{x}$$

$$x = \frac{1.3}{\tan 57}$$

5. The function $\sin 2x$ moves twice as fast as the function $\sin x$. For example, if $x = 45°$, $\sin x = \sin 45 = \frac{\sqrt{2}}{2}$ and $\sin 2x = \sin 90 = 1$. So $\sin 2x$ reaches its maximum at half the angle at which $\sin x$ reaches its maximum. Sin x reaches its maximum, 1, at $\frac{\pi}{2}$; $\sin 2x$ reaches its maximum at half of that, $\frac{\pi}{4}$.

6. 6.28 is about 2π, so 6.28 radians is one cycle of $y = \sin\theta$. Changing $y = \sin\theta$ into $y = A\sin\theta$ changes only the curve's height. The only answer shown that differs from the curve of $y = \sin\theta$ only in height is A.

7. $\tan = {}^{opposite}/_{adjacent}$ The tangent of angle A is equal to the length of side CB divided by the length of side AC. To find that, you have

to find the length of side *AC*. Pythagorean Theorem time again.

$$13^2 = 12^2 + \overline{AC}^2$$

$$\overline{AC}^2 = 13^2 - 12^2$$

$$\overline{AC}^2 = 169 - 144$$

The length of *AC* is 5 and tan *A* is 12/5.

13407842R00027

Made in the USA
Lexington, KY
30 January 2012